Tales From Templeton

Families Writing Together

Templeton Elementary School

Pen & Publish

Published by Pen & Publish
Bloomington, Indiana
(812)837-9226
Email: info@PenandPublish.com
www.PenandPublish.com

ISBN: 1-9768391-0-5
This book is printed on acid free paper.

Printed in the USA

Dedicated To Templeton Families

Acknowledgements

We want to express our appreciation to members of Bloomington Friends Meeting, Templeton neighbors, members of the Bloomington community and the Templeton Parent Teachers Organization for their financial support of this project.

We appreciate the time and energy the parents who participated in the Indiana Partnership training gave to assuring that the anthology came into being.

And, to all Templeton teachers for involving families in family literacy projects and for the wonderful teaching and mentoring they do every day.

Front Cover Birds created in John J. Audubon art class unit. Artists from left to right are :

Top: Christiana Wilkerson, Sydney Arnold, Christiana Wilkerson

Bottom: Lesley Groves, Avery Goldman, Yasha Qurashi

Front cover photograph of Faye Deckard's Kindergarten class.

Cover photographs by Dee Burt.

Drawn by Frank Leonard Templeton when he was in high school.

Templeton Elementary School is named after Frank Leonard Templeton. He was a teacher, administrator and Assistant to the Superintendent in Bloomington from 1929-1960. This letter was written by his son; Ralph Doles Templeton to his grandson, Joseph Heise, who is a student at Templeton.

Dear Joseph,

I hope you will write the story of your great-grandfather in the way you think of him. Of course, you never met him. But you know his granddaughter (your mother). And you know his son (me). We can tell you a few things about him.

Of course, I remember him as a father who taught me much of what I know and believe. He was always teaching me. He liked to build things with wood and he let me help him. He enjoyed making cabinets where we kept stuff in our house. He liked to draw. He made many of our Christmas cards. He was always singing. He had a wonderful tenor voice, and sang many solos but he couldn't read music. He taught me how important it was to be able to read music. He often led singing for groups, my job was to run the projector that showed the words to the songs. He liked fishing, and sometimes he took me with him. He was very interested in the Templeton family tree, and collected all the information he could get about all his relatives. He served in many ways the First Methodist Church, mainly as the Superintendent of the Sunday school. He taught me how to how to drive when I was much to young to get a license. He made sure I was exposed to great music at home on the radio and at concerts in the IU Auditorium when people gave me a ticket if they couldn't go. He was always arranging trips to visit relatives in wonderful places like Indianapolis, Greensburg, and Cincinnati. He liked going on Sunday "drives" to see places near Bloomington, like Brown County Park, Spring Mill Park, or the grand hotels at

French Lick and West Baden. Once at the Bloomington airport, he paid $2 for me to take a ride in a little Piper Cub airplane.

But those are not the reasons Templeton School was named after him. Others remember him for his work in the Bloomington schools. I am mailing you a couple of old newspaper articles; you should receive them in a few days. (You can keep them. I have other copies.) They tell very well why the school was named Templeton school. He started teaching in Bloomington in 1924, and he had many jobs in the schools until he retired in 1960. That's a long time—36 years! He was a teacher and administrator. (Ask your mother what that word means.) He worked on many of the changes that were needed as schools served more and more students. He helped make it possible for Bloomington to have good schools such as Templeton.

I'm sure he is smiling down on you and proud of how well you are doing at Templeton school.

Have fun telling your story.

Love, March 11, 2005

Grandpa Frank Templeton

By Janet Templeton-Heise

My grandpa died just before I turned 16. He was the first of my grandparents to pass away, so he was the one I had the least time with. But, I found out after he died that he had had a major heart attack 10 years before, so I was very grateful for those additional years to share.

One of the things I remember most about growing up was going to Grandpa and Grandma's house here in Bloomington from my home in Columbus, especially every year for the Fourth of July. Back then, the fireworks used to be in the old IU stadium that stood where the big green space and playing fields now are on 10th St. west of the Library. I remember being a little kid amongst all those big people, walking into the Stadium, and it was a huge place to me; bigger than anyplace in Columbus, anyway. All of my aunts and uncles and cousins on my dad's side were in Bloomington for the fireworks, so that was a time to have fun with cousins I didn't get to see very often. The fireworks were always wonderful; and after navigating the traffic to get back to Grandma and Grandpa's house on 1st Street, we would have sparklers in the front yard and wave to the cars passing by. The biggest treat, though, was when Grandpa piled all the kids in the car and took us to get ice cream at the Penguin, now known as the Chocolate Moose (and still one of my very favorite places!). It was always a summer weekend to play, catch "lightning bugs," and to feel special. That's the biggest gift that all my grandparents gave me -- loving me so much that I knew it without question.

Since then, in growing up, I've appreciated the gifts my grandparents gave me, all the more since they are all gone now. Here in Bloomington, my grandpa taught me about learning something every day (in school or not), and my grandma taught me that taking care of family is something done with love, and not only because it's the right thing to do. When my grandpa died, all of us cousins gathered together and sang "Turn, Turn, Turn" at his funeral, and indeed, there is a time for everything.

Fast-forwarding through the years, I could not have predicted that long after I thought I was done having children, I would move to Bloomington, fall in love with the man who is Joe's dad, and have one more son, who goes to Templeton School. My grandpa would be proud of Joe's school, and all of the special people who work there -- and that school is named after him, for his many years of service to the Bloomington community.

Thanks, Grandpa, for the gifts you gave me and many others, which live on today at (Frank L.) Templeton School.

Janet Templeton-Heise

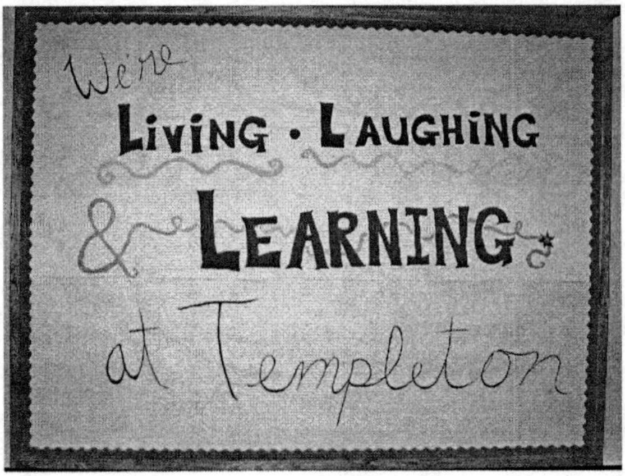

What is Family?

Written by: The Bunton Family

Family is playing outside.
Family is road trips every summer.
Family is tickle time and pillow fights.
Family is taking walks together.
Family tastes like Ritter's frozen custard.
Family smells like campfires and toasted marshmallows.
Family sounds like making up silly songs.
Family feels like hugs and kisses.
Family looks like skipping rocks across the lake.
Family makes me feel happy, safe and warm inside.
Family is Daddy, Mommy, Jon and Sammy.

Memories of Poppy Breedlove

by Valerie Breedlove and Michael Osborn

Poppy used to take Michael for rides on the lawnmower to help him fall asleep when he was an infant.

Poppy and Michael spent a lot of time doing "man things." Poppy taught Michael how to hook up a trailer and how to mow the lawn with a riding lawnmower.

When Poppy was first diagnosed with terminal cancer, Mesothelioma, he told Val that he needed a ride to the voter registration to change from a democrat to a republican. I was shocked because Poppy was a lifelong democrat. I ask him why he wanted to switch and he told me it was better for a republican to die than a democrat was.

Poppy used to take Michael of the John Deere Gator. Poppy owned lakefront property at Lake Monroe and enjoyed the chance to go up there. Poppy and Michael would drive over all sorts of things. Once they got stuck on a tree stump and had to dig their way out.

Another time on the lake land Poppy and Michael had to cut down a tree that had fallen across the trail. Their chainsaw ran out of gas so they had to chop it with axes.

We got stuck out on the water in Poppy's houseboat in a lightening storm. We could not go to the buoy because the water was too choppy. We anchored in the middle of the lake and made some romaine noodles. Good thing we had our sea legs.

THE STORY OF THE CHOCOLATE MOOSE

by the Christensen Family: Maddie, Eloise, Sarah Jane, Rob and Flori

Long ago in Bloomington, Indiana, there was a small ice cream shop for sale. An elegant mannered skunk who had inherited a fortune from her rich uncle bought the shop and painted a new sign that said "SKUNKY SPUMONI: Ice Cream and Cold Treats". It was a very nice sign and a bright, clean shop, but it didn't attract a lot of customers. Many people who stopped for a treat were quickly turned off by the skunky smell and the striped rodent scooping the ice cream. Hardly anyone

ever came and soon "SKUNKY SPUMONI" went out of business and the shop was closed again.

Next it was purchased by a Weasel family. They named the shop "THE FROSTY WEASEL". Weasels are known for being quite mean and they were often rude to the customers. If anyone complained, he or she would get an eye full of weasel spit, or even a nasty scratch or bite on the hand. Needless to say, business did not go well and soon there were no customers at all.

The ice cream shop suffered a series of unqualified owners with unfortunate management problems, including: a mouse couple who nibbled holes in all the cones, a squirrel who insisted on putting nuts in everything, a family of possums who kept turning the cones upside down and dropping ice cream on people's shoes, and a cheetah who dished ice cream so fast that it splattered all over the walls, creating a terrible, sticky mess.

Finally, an enterprising moose from nearby Yellowwood Forest purchased the shop. He saw all the mistakes that had been made in the past and thought he would be able to do a better job.

He spent three whole days just cleaning up. He made fresh ice. He bought new ice cream cones and sprayed down all the walls—washing away the weasel spit, the skunk smell, and the splattered ice cream. He mopped the floor and even repainted the ceiling.

Then he bought stone benches and napkin dispensers so people could sit and enjoy their frozen treats. All of this was easy and made good business sense. The hardest part was coming up with a new name for the shop. Moose knew that if he had a catchy name on the sign, people would stop to check it out and then remember it and come back again later.

He went back to Yellowwood to clear his mind and get some creative inspiration. Moose stopped to visit his friend, the wise old owl and ask his advice. Owl said, "I've noticed that people REALLY like chocolate, so that should definitely be part of the name."

Now, Moose was hard-working, friendly, and honest, but he was also quite vain and loved to get attention. He decided to call it "THE CHOCOLATE MOOSE". He painted a rather large portrait of himself on the sign and hung it up high where everyone could see. His hard work and good ideas paid off and "THE CHOCOLATE MOOSE" was an instant, enormous success.

The Raccoon in the Attic

by Daniel Davila

Now this might sound weird, but it's true, trust me, here it goes: It was like, August when this happened. We were hearing strange noises up in the attic. We thought it was squirrels on the roof but it wasn't. One night at 5:00 a.m. there was a giant THUD! My mom rushed upstairs to see what had happened. Dad was too scared to get out of bed and see what had happened. Lucia and I were still asleep. My mom looked. She couldn't believe it- one of the ceiling tiles had fallen down because rain had come in through a hole chewed through the roof. That's when she said, "I don't think there are squirrels on the roof, I think there's a raccoon!" So my mom set a trap and all we caught were cats, squirrels and other animals. We tried everything: bacon, peanut butter and grapes and stuff. But we couldn't outsmart the raccoon. He was too crafty. So my mom's nice to animals and so she didn't kill it. It was scaring us at night with all the dancing around and THUDS! And WHAMS! And THWACKS! And SMACKS! So we had to put a stop to this. So one day these friends came over with their mom and dad and my mom told them about the raccoon. And their dad said, "Try looking at the roof. Is there a hole there?" He said there was. Then he said, "Now cover it up with metal because that's where the raccoon must be hiding. So be careful because he can chew through wood but not through metal!" he said. We tried but unfortunately it didn't work. The raccoon just made another hole to go into. My mom kept trying but it didn't work. So finally it came to the day when you know it starts getting warm and all the animals like to be outside. Well, finally we got rid of him when it was summer and he wanted to go out there and play games with his raccoon friends and that's how we got rid of the raccoon!

The Diersing's at the Beach

by Catherine, Larry, Colin, Adam, Spencer and Eli Diersing

One of our favorite places to visit is the beach of Lake Michigan. We have had many adventures during our trips there.

Running from the Waves

One of the adventures that Eli remembers was what great fun he, Gracie and Halle had running away from the waves. We were running away from the waves and jumping on the sand, but not head first. Then we jumped and ran into the water so far we had to run fast in the sand. We showed Aunt Jenny and Uncle Rob how fast we had to go. We showed my Mommy and Halle's Mommy, Aunt Kim, and our Daddies. When we were finished we dug a hole so deep that nobody could find us in it!

The Queen of Sheba

An adventure that Adam remembers is pulling the Queen of Sheba in the blow up boat. Once upon a time, because all good stories start that way, me and Spencer were pulling the Queen Of Sheba, really Megan, in a blow up boat. We had a plan to pull Megan so fast that she would fall off of the boat. By mistake, Spencer and I tripped over each other a couple of times. Then we got back up and pulled and pulled and pulled and rocked and tipped the boat over and Megan finally fell out. Splash!!! Then, Spencer and I got up and started to surf on the blow up boat.

<u>The Treasure Hunt</u>
One thing Spencer remembers is that he and his Grandma and his Mom and his Dad made a treasure hunt. They made lots of stuff out of clay and spray painted it. Finally, when the day came, on June 24, Spencer's birthday, he and his dad and his uncles put out the clues. The treasure was in trash bags and one treasure chest. My cousins and brothers and I got bubble swords at the start of the treasure hunt. The clues were hidden under rocks, some were buried and there was a pirate flag. Under it was hidden another clue. It was a pirate flag I got for another birthday and had hanging with a ship's steering wheel on top of my bed. We burnt the edges of the clues to make them look old. We got the first clue when we were at the house we rented in Michigan. The first clue took us to the beach on the sand dunes. It was hidden under a rock. The older kids wanted to go really quickly through it while the younger kids took their time. The pirate flag was hung on a stick. We dug with oars. There were like 10 clues we had to find. One clue got a little deep where it burned so it was hard to read. Carly carried the clues. Finally when we found the treasure it was buried under the sand castle. The older kids dug it up. I remember the younger kids kind of doing it but they couldn't really do it. Once we got it we put the bubble mix into the bubble swords. You put them in the sheath and the bubbles would go streaming through when the wind blew. When we got to the house everyone was

using the treasures from the treasure hunt. You could blow bubbles off of the deck. I think it went well. Our youngest cousin, Maggie, thanked me. She said it was fun.

Scrabble Summer

One morning just after breakfast, while waiting and fantasizing about the much awaited moment when the adults would take us to the beach, we wandered into the living room attempting to explore the house which we rented. We daringly threw open the closet that we had always simply assumed was locked. This theory was proven incorrect, so we found an unlocked closet full of games. After discussion and dismissing Battleship as too complicated, we finally agreed on a simple game that we both believed to know the rules to, Scrabble. Unknowingly we played by our own rules changing several. With dictionary at hand we browsed spontaneously and with much assistance from adults passing through managed scores in the hundreds. This Scrabble expedition was not only fun but led to many more such games. One began at around seven in a parent bedroom, and lasted well into the night. This found us with many new vocabulary words, such as a Japanese instrument that by some miracle I don't recall the name of. This game, which slowly attracted all the parents present was great fun and has often been repeated. It became the summer of Scrabble for my parents and I.

The Things They Say

The adventures that I remember from these trips are the things that the nine children say when we are all together.

"The shells are the flowers of the beach."
"The waves are their mountains."
"That sunset is the doorway into heaven."
"Eli, can you teach Halle how to talk?" "Sure" as he takes Halle's hand in his and walks away from the crowd. As they go he can be heard saying, "Can you say horse? Horse, Halle, say horse."

The Anniversary and Engagement

Our trip to the beach encompasses not only Spencer's birthday, but our anniversary as well. Last year we made homemade cheesecake to be shared with all, and we took our slices to the top of the dunes to enjoy while watching the sunset. As the sun started to set, a young couple wandered down the beach hand in hand. He slowly turned to face her and as he did, we knew he was going to ask her to marry him. He lowered himself to one knee and from far away, we could sense the emotion on both of their young faces. He took her hands, he gave the ring; she nodded yes and their friends came running in celebration. A great affirmation of our anniversary.

Sidewalks

Meg, Addison and Madeline Elkins

It was a warm May day on the campus of the University of Notre Dame. In a small chapel, sunlight streamed through the stained glass windows bathing Theresa's wrinkled skin and white hair in light as she sat in her wheelchair wearing her favorite color purple. Surrounded by five generations of her family gathered to celebrate her 100th birthday, Theresa listened to the priest, Father Douglas, talk about the many inventions she had witnessed during her lifetime. Airplanes, radios, DVD players, the Space Shuttle and much much more during the past 100 years.

Father Douglas then asked "Theresa, What is your favorite invention?"

"Cement sidewalks." Theresa answered.

Theresa's family began to chuckle because of her response.

"Theresa, why do you say that concrete sidewalks are you favorite invention?" Asked Father Douglas with a curious tone.

Theresa's eyes twinkled as she thought back to another one of her birthdays, this time in Moorehead Minnesota, the year 1909. It was her 7th birthday. Theresa remembers her mother in the kitchen baking her birthday cake while wearing her well worn apron that she always wore while in the kitchen.

"Mother, may I please open my presents?" begged

Theresa. Theresa was wearing her new purple gingham dress her mother had spent weeks sewing for her. Her mother completed it just in time for Theresa's birthday.

"No Theresa," responded her mother. "Your father would be very disappointed to not be able to see you open your presents."

Theresa's mother understood the unbearable anticipation Theresa was experiencing. She tried to think of an activity that would occupy Theresa for a time while she finished baking the cake.

"I know," said Theresa's mother. Mother walked over to the money jar kept high on top of the cupboard and stood on her tip toes as she reached to bring the jar down safely. Mother took two pennies from the jar and returned it to its spot. "Share one of these pennies with your brother and go down to Mr. Stull's store and buy a piece of candy. Enjoy your walk since it is such a beautiful day."

"Thank you Mother!" Theresa exclaimed as she ran out the door to find her brother Niles.

"Niles!" hollered Theresa. "I have a penny for you to spend at Mr. Stull's store!"

Ten year-old Niles was across the street playing catch with his friends. Wearing brown knickers and a white shirt with a hole in the arm, Niles walked over to his sister. Theresa gave Niles a penny.

"Then let's get going to Mr. Stull's store!" said Niles.

Niles turned and waved to his friends as Theresa and he headed for the store.

Theresa and Niles walked along the wooden sidewalks past the many familiar houses in Moorehead. They had made this journey hundreds of times running errands for their parents, walking to school, and walking to church on Sundays. They knew the walk by heart.

Theresa began to skip ahead of Niles. Niles saw a loose board on the sidewalk, but before he could yell out to Theresa he watched as she fell to the ground. Theresa was crying by the time Niles reached her side.

"Are you OK?" asked Niles.

"NO!" Theresa cried. "I lost my penny." As Theresa fell she watched helplessly as her penny rolled through a crack in the wooden sidewalk.

"Let's see if we can find it." said Niles.

Theresa and Niles began to look through the cracks in the wooden sidewalk. Niles spotted the penny shimmering near a puddle beneath a board. Niles tried to reach his hand through the crack, but his hand was too big.

"Theresa, you try to reach the penny with your hand." Niles said.

Theresa tried as hard as possible to reach her penny, but then she started crying when she realized she couldn't reach the penny either.

In a flash Niles was off to the woodshed behind his house to retrieve his father's ax. Theresa was so upset that she hadn't even noticed Niles had left and returned with the ax.

"Stand back Theresa." Niles instructed.

To Theresa's amazement Niles began to chop away at the sidewalk. After about 10 whacks to the sidewalk he was able to pry the board up for Theresa to reach the penny.

"Oh, thank you Niles!" Theresa exclaimed.

Relieved to have the penny back Theresa and Niles ran to Mr. Stull's store where Theresa bought the best piece of candy she had ever tasted.

A warm smile suddenly appeared on Theresa's face as she looked towards Father Douglas and said, "Because when I was a kid I dropped a penny between a crack in a wooden sidewalk and my brother chopped up the sidewalk."

Then they all ate cake and cheered!

I love Sledding

by Addison Elkins

Do you
Like sledding?

Well I do
I do

Just like
To go down

The hill
anyone

Like
But the best Part

About
Sledding

Is falling off the
The sled

And feeling
The iciness
Of the snow
In your face!

A Story by Carmen Garcia

Mi Aabuelito

Mi abuelito era un hombre muy trabajador el trabajaba cuidando sus vacas y otras mas de otras personas. Cuando el salía para el campo con el ganado de vacas mi abuelita los encaminaba. Y un día cuando ella regresaba para la casa se le apareció la Llorona. Por donde ellos vivían estaba cerca de un arrollo y ella vio una mujer con un pelo muy largo y vestida de blanco y oyó que gritaba muy feo. Ella se asusto tanto que se enfermo. Pero, gracias a dios ella se recupero. Todavía viven y yo Edgar me gustaría mucho poder platicar con mis bisabuelos pero ya siquiera los conocí. Mi abuelita nos mando un video de ellos y ya están muy viejitos. Apenas se caminan.

My Grandfather

by Carmen Garcia

My grandfather was a hard-working man and worked taking care of his cattle and cattle belonging to other people. When he would leave to go to the pastures with his cattle my grandmother would walk with him. One day when she was coming back home "la Llorona" appeared before her. They lived close to a creek and she saw a woman with very long hair dressed in white and she heard her screaming horribly. She was so scared that she got sick. But, thank God, she recovered. They are still alive and I, Edgar, would really like to talk to my great-grandparents but at least I got to see them. My grandmother sent us a video of them and they are really old. The can hardly walk.

My Dad, The Stranger in Town

Written and inspired by
Beth Isom, Jamie and Shannon Murphy

What an awesome day! Blue skies, no school and my fishing pole. Nothing stopping me now. I can see my favorite fishing spot from here. All I have to do is plop this pole in the pond and watch those Bluegills come, I thought, planting myself down on my favorite spot. It's going to be a great day!

"Daniel, I have a letter. I think you may want to open it right away." My grandma handed it to me and hiked back up the hill to the cabin. I looked at my name on the front, Daniel Bowen. I turned it over and looked at the name on the back.

"Sam Bowen. Holy cow, Sam Bowen is my dad's name." I sprang to my feet and ran like a mad man to the cabin. I crashed through the screened door. It slammed shut behind me. My heart felt like it was going to burst through my chest. My tongue seemed like it was stuck to the roof of my mouth. I couldn't even speak or swallow. I thought I might spontaneously combust.

"Are you okay, Daniel?" Grandma asked softly. "You don't look so good. Honey, sit down. Let me get you some water."

I sat down. My hands were red and shaky as I handed her the envelope.

"Do you want me to read it?" she asked as she took it from me.

All I could manage to do was gulp down the water. I felt like I was going to die. Finally I managed to shake my head "yes."

She carefully opened the envelope with a kitchen knife and pulled out one single sheet of white paper. I intensely watched her eyes move left to right.

"Well!" I blurted out, throwing my arms up in the air. Finally, I had words again.

"It says your dad is going to be in town tomorrow and if you want to see him, he'll be at the Country Diner at noon. That's pretty much it," she told me.

"Twelve years he's been MIA and that's it? Great. I guess he just wants me to drop everything," I spouted at the top of my lungs. I pushed myself away from the table and stomped off to my room. Grandma didn't say one word.

I lay on my bed and stared at the rafters. My brain was a train wreck, a million thoughts at once. I turned over on my side and leaned on my elbow.

"This is crazy," I said to the picture of my mom that sits on my night stand.

"Why now? Why? Now I have a gigantic decision to make, and no time to make it. What a jerk he is. How could any man just leave his family like that? And the bum didn't even go to your funeral, Mom. How rude is that? He is probably a chain-smoking drunk, or worse, a druggie. He's probably never set one foot in a church. And the worse thing of all, Mom, I think I want to meet him. I must be nuts!" I turned her picture face down, even though I know she can't hear me or help me.

I sat in my room all day. The day turned into evening and the evening into night. I tossed and turned all night, until my bed covers were twisted and knotted up. I closed my eyes for a minute, trying to trick myself into sleep, but it didn't work.

Grandma came up to my room the next morning and gently knocked on my door. I bolted up in bed. I must have finally dozed off.

"Daniel," she said, "will you come down to breakfast? "

"Oh, um, give me a minute. I'll be down," I said quickly. I slipped into slippers and scooted to my bathroom. I looked in the mirror, and to my horror I looked like I hadn't slept in weeks. My eyes were bloodshot. My thick hair was wadded and turned up like someone had sucked it in a vacuum sweeper. Oh, this is great. I look as bad as I feel. I brushed my teeth, and the butterflies started swarming in my guts. I finally made it down stairs to breakfast and tried to eat. Nibbling on the edges of some wheat toast, I could feel my grandparents' eyes on me. They were waiting for my big decision. "Okay, I'm going," I said softly.

Now I have to get ready to meet my dad. So, just what do you wear to meet your dad for the first time? I didn't have a clue. A shirt and tie; I don't think so. Shorts and a tank top? Not so good either. I finally gave up and just sat on my bed. Somehow I managed the strength to take a shower and get dressed. Finally, it was time to go. I watched the telephone poles pass by at incredible speeds. It made me sort of sick, so I looked away. We rode silently all the way there. Before I was ready, we were there. Grandma pulled the car to the curb in front of the diner. "Daniel, are you sure you want to go through with this?" Her voice sounded a little shaky.

"Yep, a man has to do what a man has to do!" I said, pretending to be brave, pretending I was really a man. Pretending my knees weren't knocking.

I somehow managed to open the door and get out of her car. I stood frozen, staring at the diner door. I never noticed how big that door was before. All that was between me and that door was four or five feet and two concrete steps. I walked up to the window and peered inside. My eyes scanned the faces of the people in the diner. Did anyone look like me? There was an old couple at a table. A young girl reading a book in a booth. A family laughing and talking to each other. I could see the waitresses. Wait, there was a man sitting at a table all by himself, facing the door. Could that be my dad? Man, what am I doing here? I must be crazy. The man glanced up from his cup he was holding and peered in my direction. He had a black jacket and a white collar on. No way, that can't be him! That can't be my dad. He looks like a preacher. The man's eyes locked onto mine. His mouth grew into a huge smile. Was he smiling at me? I looked over my shoulder. There wasn't anybody behind me.

"Oh my God," I said out loud. He got up from his table and walked in my direction to the door. He pulled the diner door open. My heart was beating like a bass drum.

"Hi, Daniel," he said, still grinning. "I'm your dad. But you can call me Sam, if you'd be more comfortable. I've been waiting a long time for this day." A gigantic smile crept over my face,

"Me too, Dad. Me too!" I guess some people do change.

Hidden Treasures

Written and inspired by
Beth Isom and Jamie & Shannon Murphy

Man, oh man! I am so glad it is almost the weekend. Only seven more days to the Thunder Over Louisville. If only grandma wouldn't drive me crazy with those stupid garage sales every Saturday. How can anyone like garage sales so much? It must be a "girl" thing. Don't get me wrong. My grandma isn't old or anything like that. She is pretty cool for her age. But give a guy a break; garage sales every freakin' Saturday. At least next Saturday I will be spared. It's Thunder weekend. Grandpa and Grandma never miss the Thunder.

Sometimes I just sit around and wonder what it would be like if my parents were around. What would my life be like? Grandma has tons of pictures of mom around. Yeah, she died when I was three. I can't say I really remember her 'cause I really don't. I look close up in the mirror sometimes, but I don't really see her in me. My hair is thick and brown. Hers was thin and blond. She was pretty skinny, but she was sick so you can't really go by that much. I may have her nose. It was sort of skinny with a slope like mine. Maybe I look like my dad? He ran off before I was born. Grandma says he had brown hair too. Maybe freckles on his nose, but she can't really remember because it has been too long. Oh well, maybe one day he will come back to see how I turned out? I'm sure not holding my breath about that one.

Well, I better turn off my light before Grandma sees it. Oh joy, another garage sale tomorrow. It will be here before I want it to that's for sure.

Wow! Grandma was right. She always says, "You just never know what treasures you might find at a garage sale." The first house we stopped at was having a moving sale. The family is moving because the Dad is getting shipped out to fight in some war somewhere. I couldn't believe my eyes when I saw the brand new football still in the box. And those cool Walkie Talkies just sitting there on the table. They only used them a couple of times and the batteries were still good. Sweet! Now I am so ready for the Thunder. I can't wait to tell my cousin Tyler. He is going to freak!

La Familia Rodríquiz Martínez

by Rosa Rodriquez
Leonardo and Erika Avila

Nosotros somos la familia Rodríguez Martínez. Está formada por Javier papá, Norma mamá, Javi y Pedro Félix. Ahora somos cuatro en la familia pero hubo un tiempo en que fuimos cinco. Teníamos una perrita que se llama Cessna. Le pusimos ese nombre porque a todos los hombres de la casa les gustan los aviones y Cessna es una marca de avioneta. Cessna es una Golden Retriever y nació en octubre de 1998. Nosotros la compramos en diciembre y tenía dos meses. Javi jugaba mucho con ella y Pedro Félix le tenía un poquito de miedo. Cessna era muy buena con los niños y todos los vecinitos iban a jugar con ella. Cuando vivíamos en ciudad Juárez, estábamos en una casa con patio y ahí tenía su casita. Cessna pero luego nos tuvimos que mandar a El Paso, Texas a un departamento y no podimos llevarla con nosotros. La tuvimos que relegar a una amiga que quiere mucho a los perros. Aunque todos estábamos muy tristes sabemos que su nueva dueña la iba a querer mucho. Cuando ya vivíamos en El Paso, dos veces la fuimos a visitar. La Cessna se veía feliz. Los niños la extrañan mucho y siempre la vamos a recordar con cariño.

The Rodriguez Martinez Family

by Rosa Rodriquez
Leonardo and Erika Avila

We are the Rodriguez Martinez family. In our family there is Javier, dad; Norma, mom, Javi and Pedro Felix. Now we are a family of four, but there used to be five of us. We had a little dog named Cessna. We named her that because all the men in the house like airplanes and a Cessna is a kind of small plane. Cessna is a Golden Retriever and was born in October 1998. We bought her in December when she was two months old. Javi played a lot with her and Pedro Felix was a little afraid of her. Cessna was really good with the children and all the neighbor kids came to play with her. When we lived in Ciudad Juarez, we had a house with a patio and that's where Cessna had her dog house. But then we had to move to El Paso, Texas, to an apartment and we couldn't take her with us. We had to give her to a friend who would love her well. When we were living in El Paso we went to visit her twice. Cessna seemed happy. The children miss her a lot and we will always remember her with love.

The Ocean

by Noah-3, Laura-5, Jenn & Kyle Marcum
Illustrated by Laura Marcum

Once there was a kid going to get some water from the ocean and he saw a fish.

So, he put his foot in the ocean to catch the fish and a turtle nibbled on his little piggies. (Or toes as mommies and daddies call them.) Then he giggled and called his mother to tell her the story and said "I love you" before he hung up.

Again, he put his foot in the ocean to catch the fish and a seahorse came by and licked his foot. Then he cried tears of joy and called his father to tell him the story and said "I love you" before he hung up.

And again, he put his foot in the ocean to catch the fish and a fish sniffed his foot and swam away. By that time the little boy had figured out that he needed a better way to catch the fish. So, he went home to get a net.

The boy returned a few minutes later to discover that the fish had went home to see his mother and father because he loved them just as much as the boy loved his.

McMillian Memories

by Will, JD, Jeff and Deb McMillian

We have so many funny, wonderful family memories that we can't pick our favorite! We have memories that Grandma and Grandpa, mom and dad and Aunt Jane and Uncle Greg share with us. We even have memories of our dog.

Our favorite memory from Grandma and Grandpa is about grandma's 1936 Chevy which Grandpa sunk in the lagoon at Sinnissippi Park. Grandpa was sliding on the ice, broke a tie rod and when he left the car on the ice it warmed up and the car sank!!! Our Grandpa likes to tell us about the pet pig he had when he was a boy; the pig's name was Betsy. Grandpa's sister, our Aunt Betsy does not think this is funny. We love to go to Chicago with our Grandma because she used to live there in 1957. Grandma tells us lots of stories about the things she used to do in Chicago. She told us about sliding down the banister at the Chicago Theater and one time we went there so we could slide down too.

Dad tells us stories about himself, Aunt Jane and Uncle Greg when they were all little. Aunt Jane and Uncle Greg tell us stories too and then they all say that the other is fibbing! Dad also tells us great stories about Grandma Joy and Grandpa John. Dad laughs about the way Grandpa John combed his hair over to the side to hide his bald spot. (We think dad will have to do this too some day). Dad also says that Grandma Joy made the best cookies. He found some three years after Grandma Joy passed away and they still tasted good. We have a very special memory of our Great Grandma Nelle. She lived in Charleston, WV. When she would get hungry she would say, "I'm so hungry I could eat the butt end out of a skunk!" The first time Will and JD heard this they laughed and laughed.

Mom's favorite memories are about when we were little. She always likes to remind us about JD's nick name for Will (Beeya) and how Will took Chip the Bear all the way to Colorado on the airplane. Mom also likes to remind Will of the day he opened the camera and ruined all the pictures taken in the delivery room on the day that JD was born.

We used to have a dog named Worf. He was a funny dog who would play fetch for hours. One day he was playing in the snow and he ran over our cousin, Candice. Candice got really mad and then before she could get out of the way Worf ran over her again!!! Worf also stole a chocolate croissant right out of mom's hand one day. Instead of running away with it, he just sat there and pretended that he had nothing in his mouth!

We have lots of camping memories. We have camped in a tent, a pop-up camper and a travel trailer. We camp with all of our friends and we go fishing, and hiking, we ride bikes and build fires, we catch crawdads and have treasure hunts. We really like to celebrate birthdays at the campground.

One of dad's favorite memories is about Will when he was little. Grandma took Will to the grocery store. While in the frozen food section, Will started taking boxes of frozen food out of the freezer and putting them on the floor. Then he began stomping on them. Grandma didn't know why he was doing this. Then she remembered, that is how Grandpa taught Will to recycle empty boxes.

One of dad's favorite memories is about JD when he was little. We had purchased the huge 4 pound box of animal crackers at Sam's. Some how JD managed to get the container out of the pantry and into the bathroom, where he dumped the entire 4 pounds of animal crackers into the toilet. Lucky for us, he didn't flush.

These are only some of our favorite memories and we have many, many, many more memories yet to come!

Andrew

by Jayna Mirer, Andrew's mother

Andrew enjoys many things in life in and out of school. As you know Andrew enjoys all types of music. He enjoyed classical, rock, contemporary Christian, Celtic, jazz, children's, and the odd such as Spike Jones and the Muppets. Andrew spends a lot of time at home lying in his bed listening to music and his siblings playing. He laughs throughout the day and really enjoys the attention of others. He goes to his brother's basketball games and baseball fames. Andrew is often a "jungle gym" for his younger sister. She likes to set next to him and talk away and he just smiles and listens. Andrew goes to church weekly and enjoys the interaction with the people there. He often grins when they talk to him. He likes to visit his grandparents at their home and likes to ride in the van. In the summer he enjoys swimming in his grandparent's swimming pool or his aunt's. On occasion Andrew will wrestle with his grandfather and brother, smiling and laughing throughout.

When he was smaller he thoroughly enjoyed playing tag. His father would hold him and run chasing his older brother. Now that he is so big they play tag as Andrew is pushed about in his wheelchair, outdoors. It is hard for Andrew to enjoy the slide at the park because he needs a lot of help. But the park is still pleasurable to Andrew. We set out a sleeping bag beneath the shade of a tree and Andrew lies there with his Mom or Dad listening to the birds, the breeze through the leaves and the joyful sound of children playing. He often laughs at the sounds and the feel of the breeze across his body. Andrew has helped our family enjoy the simple pleasures in life, we are so blessed to have Andrew in our lives.

(Andrew is a delightful 9 year old boy with Cerebral Palsy. He has been coming to Templeton since 1999).

A Cow Eats Butter: A Story from my Father

by Tsering Palzom

It was a very sunny day. In the Mountains of Tibet our family camped there to look after animals. We have about 300 yaks and 200 sheep, and a few horses. My father and mother went in the Mountains with the animals. My sister and I had to stay home in order to guard the tent. There is a cow who broke her leg and cannot join the other animals. The cow and us played together around the tent. Between the games we did not pay attention to the cow. My sister and I continuously played the game. When we came back to the tent, the cow ate all the butter. Then my parents came back from the Mountains. When they saw the cow eating butter they were surprised and told us never let cows eat butter again.

Una Historia por Cristina Pérez

Todos los días cuando ya teníamos le edad de cocinar y preparar el café y el almuerzo lo hacíamos turnándonos. Mi hermana y yo, nos levantamos a las 6:00 de la mañana. Tendíamos nuestra cama y nos vestíamos con el uniforme para la escuela. El café se lo llevamos al buró de la recamara de mis tíos. Mi tía nos preparaba el jugo de naranja, zanahoria, betabel, licuado de plátano o de papaya. Mi tía nos varía los desayunos y nosotros aprendimos buenas cosas. Después nos íbamos a la escuela caminando para llegar a la escuela a las 8:00 de la mañana. Yo viví más tiempo con mis tíos y fue muy hermoso y los extraño mucho.

A Story by Cristina Pérez

Each day when we were old enough to cook and make coffee and lunch we did this by taking turns. My sister and I would get up at 6:00 a.m. We made our bed and we got dressed in our school uniforms. We took the coffee in to the dresser in my aunt and uncle's bedroom. Mi aunt would prepare orange, carrot, beet and juice, and banana or papaya smoothies. Mi aunt made us a variety of breakfasts so we learned good habits. Then we would walk to school arriving at 8:00 a.m. I lived longer with my aunt and uncle and it was really wonderful- I miss them a lot.

My Family

by Ramona Puello & Jasely

My family is very small. In my family is my grandma, my mom, my dad and my grandpa. My dad and my grandpa don't live with me. My dad lives in New York City. My grandpa lives in Dominican Republic "Santiago". Though they live far away we keep in touch. I have family everywhere. Some line in New York City, some live in Santo Domingo. I love my family very much and they love me too.

The Milky Way Museum

by Jill, Aaron, James and Kara Rogers

One time I jumped from an airplane and decided to open up my parachute. I didn't want to go down, so I turned on my rockets, put away my parachute, and went up to space. When I was up in space, I didn't need a helmet. I finally spotted the Milky Way and headed straight to it. While I was up in the Milky Way, there was a city made of stars. I looked like Indianapolis. The people were ordinary humans and their clothes were rocks and stars – men with rocks, women with stars.

I spotted an art museum, and being an artist myself, I decided to go in. Inside, it was like a chapter book, with different art from different times. Some artwork was made of stone, some of wood. There were big masks of all kinds with different expressions.

There was a whole section of art by children. The artwork was amazing! Mrs. Bernstein, was the art teacher of some of the students whose art was displayed. One of the art pieces was about a mermaid trying to help her friends. The friends were going to be eaten by big fish without the help of the mermaid. When I looked closely, I notice that the artist was ME!

Poetry in Our Lives

by The Rogers: Jill, Aaron, Kara and Josh

Driving through the national park
Elk bugling from the mountains and fields,
leaping across the road
Excitement over Grandpa coming to visit
Learning new things at school and with friends
Kittens doing funny things like showering with Mom,
and falling into trashcans
Dogs always by your side,
cats guarding bedroom doors
Looking at all the seals in San Francisco
– stinky and noisy!
Gift shops full of sea creatures made into toys
Grandad's horses always reacting like a mirror to you
Indianapolis – statues and buildings like mountains
Mackinaw fireworks and big boat rides

My Trip to Mexico

by Rosa Rodriquez
Erika and Leo Auila

When we went to Mexico my mom and I went to buy tortillas. I was looking at the cows and then I stepped on a dog's tail. Then the dog got scared and mad and chased me in the backyard. This is the reason I don't want to go to Mexico because of the dogs. Another thing that scared the children was the scorpions. There are a lot of scorpions in Mexico, very poisonous. Their sting hurts very much.

Family de Santiago a collection of stories

by Elva de Santiago,
Osiel & Maria Santiago

When we came to Mexico five years ago I turned three years. My mom and dad made a cake and Osiel and my cousin turned off my candles. I cried and I was mad and my mom told the boys to stop and I was kind of happy now.

•

When we were in Mexico I was really naughty. We had a dog and a pig. I liked to ride the pig. One day I rode on the pig and the pig ran through the cactuses and thorns were all over me.

When I came home my mom was really frightened because I cried really loud and she took the thorns off of me.

Emily Shin's Family

by Emily Shin

After departing from Seoul, Korea, it took eleven hours to get to Chicago and one more hour to get to Indianapolis. We took a limousine to our apartment in Bloomington. Our apartment is very big.

We will go back to Korea this summer. When we are there we will live in our new nice apartment. Our apartment has two playgrounds. In our apartment there are two bathrooms, three bedrooms, a big living room and a cozy kitchen. In front of our apartment there are mountains. On weekends I can climb up the mountains with my family. I will go to Su-Sack Elementary School. I will be in third grade. I might be the best English speaker in the school. Now I miss my friends. I want to go to Korea soon! I have enjoyed the USA very much.

Story

by Becca Smith, Age 4 ½

Sam Smith's sister

Once there was a giraffe and she had a picnic with a wombat. They ate a salad sandwich with tomatoes and lettuce. There was only one sandwich for the giraffe because the wombat had one before and he didn't like it. The wombat had bananas, 'cause he was used to them. There were 6 bananas for the wombat. They were good but he didn't like the peels. He ate one before and he didn't like it (the peel of a banana).

The owners of the rainforest, (and of the wombat) found where they were eating. There were two walkways but they didn't know which one to go on and they went on the wrong one. That was lucky for the wombat.

"Come on" said the giraffe. The way was easy to follow cause the trail went North. So the animals were friends. The wombat would tell the giraffe where his home was. The giraffe told the wombat where her home was too. The wombat's was North and the giraffe's was South.

And they met a new friend. Their friend's name was Mary. She was 7 years old. She was a person. She took the animals home. She met them before. She was their owner before but she let them go.

Mary lived in North Carolina. She put them in a zoo. The animals were thinking about her. But she really was on a trip, and didn't come back for 5 years. When she came back from her trip Mary went to the zoo. She saw their cages, and they were back inside. When the giraffe and the wombat saw Mary, they put their arms out to hug her. The zookeepers opened the cage to let the animals out to hug Mary. Usually the zookeepers would stop the animals from running away, but they had been in the zoo for 5 years and when Mary came back they let the animals go home with her.

Jokes

by Sam Smith; First Grade

Knock, Knock.
Who's there?
Tiger
Tiger who?
Tiger Woods.

Why did the turtle cross the road?
To get to shells.

Why did the potato have eyes?
So he could have a brain.

Why did the grasshopper have legs?
So that he could hop.

Why did the ancient mummy say boo?
Because he wanted to scare you.

Why did a clarinet have a reed stuck in it?
So it could sing.

Joke

retold by Sam Smith; First Grade

How far can you walk into the woods?
Half way.
If you walk more you'd be walking out of the woods.

Boys versus Girls, and Puppies?

by Carol, Katherine, Lauren and Ben Sylvester

On the Templeton Playground a strange phenomenon has developed. It is really a great thing. Children of all ages are playing, and having lots of fun. It has been a little confusing for the supervisors though. Boys versus Girls tag sounds pretty clear to me. I would expect to see a group of boys trying to tag a group of girls, and vice versa. Makes sense doesn't it?

One day as I was walking a group of children out to the playground a little boy ran past yelling "Let's go kick the girls' butts!" I would normally be concerned but feeling certain he was talking about tag, and smug in my knowledge of the game I knew he wasn't really going to hurt anyone. I took him aside, and gently reminded him that while I understood his enthusiasm, he could possibly express himself in a gentler way. I felt I was really starting to get the hang of this playground supervisor job.

The problem came when a child approached me one day saying the girls were cheating. I walked over to a group of children and tried to find out the rules and how the girls were cheating. A little boy was explaining things to me and I became even more confused. He was complaining about the boys cheating. I said "aren't you on their team?" Apparently not, he's a girl. Not really a girl mind you, just playing on the girls' team. This kind of made me wonder why they didn't just call it plain old tag then. I didn't have time to contemplate that because the next thing really stumped me.

Apparently there are puppies involved somehow. I was

no longer feeling quite so sure of myself. How could puppies be involved in boys versus girls tag? Well, evidently the girls were puppy guarding which is strictly prohibited. You can see my confusion, if a boy can be a girl, and a girl can be a boy, can a boy be a puppy too? Puppy guarding is the act of staying too close to the jail that the tagged boy or girl is standing in, thus keeping friends from rescuing them from their predicament. I agreed that the girls were definitely cheating, even the ones who were boys. That resolved, I am still not sure why it is called boys versus girls tag, or why puppy guarding is called that. However, I am greatly enjoying working with all of your wonderful children, whether they are boys, girls, or even puppies.

Summer of the Puppies

by Bill, Carol, William, Katherine, and Lauren Sylvester

Hi, my name is Katherine, and I am 8 years old. I have a big brother William, and little sister Lauren. Lauren doesn't remember the summer of the puppies; she was only 2½ months old. We tell her about it a lot. Now I would like to tell you.

It all began on June 5 of 1999. My dad was fishing, and my Mom was getting us ready for bed. Our dog Fisher was acting funny. She was pacing around and my mom noticed some strange green liquid on the floor. The breeder we got Fisher from said she was ready to deliver her puppies. Mom was worried. She had never done this, and was home alone with three kids, and a pregnant dog.

Our neighbor Larry volunteered to ride down to the lake and find our dad. Mom was extremely grateful. Larry rode out to the lake, and walked around in the dark calling my dad's name. It's a good thing we knew the general area he was in! Unfortunately, when Larry finally found dad, his motorcycle wouldn't start, and he had to ride home with Dad.

Mom let us stay up to watch the first puppy being born. They were small and slimy. In the morning, Fisher had delivered 9 puppies. They looked very cute once she had cleaned them all up. There were 5 black, 3 yellow, and one brown puppy. They could barely walk and cry to find Mom for food.

Over the months of June and July they grew quickly. Our neighbors all watched for the puppies to come out. They looked like a heard running around our yard. They played, slept and ate. At first we could hold them in our hands, then our arms, laps, and soon they would not be held. They nipped at my hair, and ran after my brother and me as we played.

The puppies had a special friend who would come to play. Caleb the Saint Bernard was a huge dog that lived a few houses away. He would get so exited when he saw the puppies, but he was too big to play with them. Caleb would run up and sniff them, and then pounce around the yard. He was so gentle and sweet to the puppies; my mom still gets tears in her eyes when she talks about it. As the puppies grew, I got to see them open their eyes, walk, run, and begin to eat solid foods. I helped to clean them, and catch them when one would make a break for it. We fell in love with each of them, and cried as each went on to a new home.

That summer all our neighbors came around more. Everyone wanted a part of the fun. It brought us all closer together, and helped us become friends with our new neighbors. I don't know if I will ever see puppies being born again. That summer will be with me the rest of my life. Fisher was a wonderful mother, and her puppy Roscoe still lives on our street with the new neighbors we met that year. I hope all of you get to have a "summer of the puppies" at least once in your lives.

Alien Invasion

by Margaret Anne Traas

Chapter One
When it all Started

Once upon a time there was an alien named Harold. One day Harold's mom and dad told him that it was time for his first invasion mission. He asked what planet he had to invade. They said, "You have to invade Earth."

"Ok, I will get the big ship so I can invade Earth. When I get back, can we have a party?" Harold asked. "Well, I won't let you down."

When Harold set off to invade he saw Earth was really big. When he was looking at Earth there was a big crash. Harold looked up and saw he was in the middle of a meteor shower. He tried to steer his ship but it was too late. Another meteor hit the ship. The ship started to fall and with a big thump the ship started to fall with a big thump and crashed.

Two kids named Kayla and Mike heard the ship crash in the woods. They ran to see what it was. When they got to the spot where the ship crashed they saw Harold, the Alien. Then Kayla and Mike started screaming. Then they ran. When they got out of the woods, they ran into their house and stayed there for the rest of the day.

Chapter Two
Night Fall

That night Harold saw the house that Mike and Kayla ran into. He opened the door and went upstairs. There he found Mike and Kayla fast asleep. Then Harold tripped on a toy and fell to the ground. All of a sudden, Mike woke up and started screaming. Then Mike slid under Mike's bed because he heard someone coming.

Mike's mom opened the door and asked, "What's wrong with you."

"Um, I had a bad dream."

"Well, if you need anything, just call."

"Ok, I will."

"Oh, try not to wake up your sister."

"Fine, I won't wake her up."

That morning when everyone was still asleep Mike woke

up under his bed. Guess what he found. He found Harold sleeping like a baby. Mike woke Kayla up and showed her the alien. "I think we should get a rope and tie him up."

"Ok, that is the only way we can hold it anyway. After that we can burn it."

"Well, I think that is going too far."

"Fine, I won't burn him but what will we do with him?"

"I don't know. Maybe we should take it back to its broken ship."

"That's a great idea but I think we should throw it in the pond and see if it will float."

"No, we don't want to kill it."

"Why not?"

"Because his friends and family will probably try to take over the world."

"Oh, I see."

Chapter Three
He Awakes

That afternoon in the woods Harold the alien woke up. Kayla and Mike jumped up and said, "He awakes! It's a miracle!"

"Well. What do you expect? I am an alien", said Harold. Then when Mike and Kayla were talking Harold said, "Will you please be quiet?"

"What is your name?" asked Kayla.

"My name is Harold, the alien but you can call me Harold. What are your names?" Harold asked.

"Why should we tell you?" asked Mike.

"Here I'll tell you our names," said Kayla.
"No, don't tell him our names."

"Why not? We don't know him. He told us his name so I am going to tell him our names. My name's Kayla and this is my twin brother, Mike."

"Now, what should we do with Harold?"

"Here, I know", said Kayla and she grabbed a box and locked Harold in it.

Mike said, "Why did you do that?"

"Well, I wanted him to stay put while we look at his ship", she said. Then they heard their mom call, "It's time for lunch."

Mike went over to the box and said, "I'll come back and set you free after lunch."

When Mike was done eating he started to run for the

door when his mom said, "Where are you going?"

"I'm going outside."

"No, you are not. You have to go help your sister clean the room."

"Fine, I will help only if I get to go when I'm done."

"OK, you'll be able to go outside."

Chapter Four
Friends

Once Mike was done with the cleaning he raced outside into the woods and opened the box. When he opened it Harold was gone. Mike looked everywhere for him but he was nowhere to be found. Mike decided to take a break by the creek and, guess who he found. There was poor Harold sitting there all by himself.

Mike asked, "What's wrong?"

Then Harold said, "My mom and dad want me to take over the world but I can't and don't want to do it. If I don't my parents will be mad."

"Well, I think you should call them up and tell them you can't do it," said a voice from behind them. It was Kayla.

Mike asked, "When did you get here?"

"When he started his story. Why are you helping him

when you locked him in a box?"

"The only reason I did that was I thought it would kill us."

"Well, I think Harold is a nice alien. We should be friends with him."

"Ok, let's be friends with him. He can live on our shed and eat our food." Harold said,

"No, I can't stay here. Once I fix my ship I have to go home to my planet."

"Where is your home planet?"

"I live on the moon. Soon, I am going to be the King."

"Well, when you leave we will miss you a lot."

Chapter Five
Goodbye

That day Harold had finished fixing his ship and was ready to leave. Before he left Kayla asked, "Maybe you can stay one more night?"

"I wish I could. Well, goodbye."

When he landed on the moon he told his parents he didn't blow up Earth. His parents said, "You passed the test. You were never to blow up Earth." Harold was happy. He passed the test.

Cat Named Beto

by Luis Valdovinos

I have a cat names Beto. He is funny and cute. He has white hair and blue eyes. One time I was doing my homework and I saw an Airplane, no, superman, no, it's a cat! Shhhh ah Mom!! He scratched my back you cannot imagine how much I cried. And my mom just laughed at me. I still love Beto even though he is still mean to me.

The Creek

by Wilma Wampler,
with the help of Zachary Emswiller, age 8

The snow was slowly melting and going down the hill in the back yard flowing into the creek. The water in the creek was beginning to fill up faster and faster. The water was going up the hill filling up the backyard with water. Dad went to town after sandbags to stop the water from getting into the basement of the house. Jackie the little boy who had built the snowman was watching his snowman melting away. Jackie would run from window to window to watch the snowman and the melting snow filling up the creek in the back yard. Dad drove up with the bags of sand to put around the house to keep the water out of the house.

Mom was getting every thing up high so the water could not reach it. The men had come to help dad lay the sand bags around the house. The water from the creek kept getting higher and closer to the house. Jackie had never seen the water fill up the back yard so high and so close to the house. The water was higher and higher...the snow kept on melting and melting. Mom was so glad that she had boxed up all the things on the ground floor and set them up high so the water could not get in and ruin them. It was late mom said it was time for bed. Every one was putting on their P.J. and washing their teeth and turning out lights and giving good night kisses and going to bed.

The next day was so exciting, when they looked out the window the water had gone down a lot the creek was still a little bit high on the banks but it was going down!! Jackie was so happy, now he could go out on the back patio and watch the water go down. The next day the creek was down at the banks. The back yard was still very muddy no one could walk on it yet but the sun was shinning and warm and Jackie could play outside in the warm sun on the back patio.

The Day My Life Changed

by Justin Wright writing for the Wright Family

3:00 A.M., My mom went into labor and the girls were coming. My dad and I couldn't find our shoes; finally we found them side-by-side next to each other behind the Lazy-Boy. Then we were off to the hospital. 30 minutes later my mom is resting in a hospital room while my dad and I go get something to eat. When we get back to my mom's room, the doctor hands my dad the scrubs. 30 minutes later I saw my twin sisters and their names are Mary Jo Wright and Molly Wright.

Learning in the Land of Hearts

Written by:
Catherine Orzell, Christy and Sam Smith, Shaena Robertson, Colleen Rainey, Rebecca White, Bailey Hull, and Carol, Katherine, and Lauren Sylvester

SCENE 1:

Light up on Whitney Whiney sitting on the floor near her bed making Valentines. Whitney is wearing head phones and the song "Girls Just Wanna Have Fun" is heard. There is a knock at the door. Music fades but is still audible.

Mom: Whitney Whimpering Whiney! How many times have I told you to put your Valentine's away until all your homework is done?!

Mom: Whitney!! Whitney! Whitney!! WHITNEY!!!

Whitney: Hey Mom! You have to listen to this great new song by the Slackers! It's called "Homework is soooo..."
(Mom interrupts)

Mom: Whitney Whiney! You have to stop all your fiddle fussing and finish your homework!

Whitney: Awww but Moooommm! This homework isn't important! I mean, these assignments are foolish! Who care if you know to spell ballet!! *(Whitney pronounces the 't' at the end)*

Mom: (*stares*) That's Ballet (*not pronouncing the 't'*) honey...

Whitney: Oh, right. The point is I just don't have time for school. It's not important at all!

Mom: Not important?? Ms. Whiney, do you realize how important education is? Without education, you wouldn't even be able to be making those Valentines right now!

Whitney: What do you mean? I didn't learn this in school!

Mom: Sure you did! Where do you think you learned how to write and make shapes and practice coloring in the lines?

Whitney: That's fiddle fuss, Mom!

Mom: That's it Whitney. It is now officially bed time for you. If you refuse to do your homework then I refuse to let you make Valentines.

Whitney: But Mom! I'm not done yet!

Mom: Goodnight, Whitney. (*Mom exits*)
Whitney: (*to herself as she cleans up her Valentine's)* This is so unfair. Who needs school? Who needs education? Having fun is the one and only important thing. (*Whitney climbs into bed, closes her eyes, and begins to snore.)*

(Monster music music is heard. Perhaps "Monster Mash." We see "Boogie Bobby" dance, or "boogie" into Whitney's room)

(Whitney wakes up and starts to dance with Boogie Bobby and then suddenly stops)

Whitney: Oh my goodness! Who are you????

Boogie Bobby: Well I'm Boogie Bobby of course. Are you ready to bebop your way to some straight A's?

Whitney: (*rubbing her eyes)* Huh?!

Boogie Bobby: (*talking like a game show host*) Well you see Ms. Whiney, you can see that learning is fun in just a short timey. Come with me to the "Land of Hearts" and we can truly evaluate your smarts. In just a short time you'll see, how important education can really be.

Whitney: Does my mother know you're here..?

Boogie Bobby: Ha-ha hoho oh dear little one, you're mother's the one who planned this fun! Let's not waste another minute, let's start to dance. Come on Whitney, this is you're chance! I promise you, Whitney, this won't be a bore. Here we go to dance our way to knowledge's door!!

(*Whitney shrugs and begins to dance off stage with 'Boogie Bobby')*

SCENE 2:

The lights come up on "The Land of Hearts" game show just beginning. The host is introducing the contestants as game show music is heard in the background. Enter Boogie Bobby and Whitney. An audience clapping and cheering is heard in the background

Court Jester/Host: Ladies and gentlemen, boys and girls, princes and princesses, frogs and toads, welcome one and all to the "If You Listen To Your Mother, Study Really Hard, Respect Your Teachers, Do Your Homework and Learn How To Work With Other People, You'll Be A Winner Show!" I'm your host, Guessing-is-not-my-middle-name Gesture!

Whitney: (*Looking at Boogie Bobby*) You have got to be kidding me...

Boogie Bobby: Shhhh listen to what he saying, you never know who will be playing!

Court Jester: Let's meet our contestants. Contestant number one: What's your name, where are you from, and what do you think of my hair?

BBB: Bonjour! I am Beautiful Bailey Bubblegum. I am the princess here in the Land of Hearts. I just want to say I love bubblegum, I love my citizens of Hearts and I love your hair, Mr. Guessing-is-not-my-middle-name Gesture.

Whitney: Wait a second! That isn't Beautiful Bailey Bubblegum! That's Brittney Bonnet from my math class!

Boogie Bobby: So to my Whitney this girl is not what she seems, so pay close attention and watch how she'll scream!

CJ: Contestant number two, please tell us your name, where you're from, and what you think of my shoes.

Cocoa Chocolate Charlie: (*talking very very loud*) HELLLOO!! MY NAME IS COCOA CHOCOLATE CHARLIE. YOU CAN CALL ME TRIPLE C, C-SAUCE, C-MOKIN', WHATEVER YOU DESIRE. I'M FROM A REGION SOUTH OF HERE CALLED C-TOWN. YOU'RE SHOES MAN, YEAH YOUR SHOES ARE TIGHT!

Whitney: (*screams!)* That is NOT Cocoa Chocolate Charlie, nor C-sauce, nor C-mokin! That is Charlie Checkers from the 2nd grade!

CJ: (*looks at Whitney*) If our last contestant would be so kind as to step onto the stage and introduce herself.

Whitney: Who me?

CJ: Yes you!

Whitney: Couldn't be!

Boogie Bobby: Then who!

Whitney: (*stares at Boogie Bobby*) I'm sorry, what??

Boogie Bobby: It's time for a little fame with this trivia game. Answer some questions right and prizes you can claim. Don't be shy, just act cool, and use all the knowledge you learned in school!

Whitney: But..

CJ: Contestant number three. You're name, where you are from and which tie you think looks better with my hair. (*BB takes out two ties to compare. Whitney rolls her eyes and proceeds to her place on the game show*)

Whitney: (*without emotion*) My name is Whitney Whiney. I'm from Bloomington, Indiana, and I don't think either of those ties are particularly flattering on you.

CJ: Awesome! (*Awkward silence*) Is everyone ready to play "If you listen to your mother..."

All contestants: (*interrupt*) YES!

CJ: Awesome. Ms. Beautiful Bailey Bubblegum, since you are the most beautiful person in the kingdom, inside and out, you have control of the board. The categories are : Measurement, Math, Language, and a Wild Card spot. Let me remind all of you who are tuning in from home of the grand prize. Take it away Boogie.

Boogie: (looks *confused at first then proceeds*) Umm...(*looks at Whitney*) Oh that's right, I almost forgot! You win this game, you get a whole lot! No, no, it's not a pot of gold, neither a shoe with smelly mold. This prize is a favorite of Molly, Jane and Sandy. Why YES! It's a big box of Candy. (Vanna walks across the stage displaying the big box) This big chocolate heart your mouth desires, it just all depends on who's first to fire...(ssss)!

CJ: (*laughing*) AWESOME!

WW: Oh my goodness!!! OHHHHH MY GOODNESS!!! You don't understand!! That's my favorite part of Valentine 's Day! I would give ANYTHING to have that box of chocolate! I'm going to win this game...I just hope I studied enough.

CJ: Triple B, you're up!

BBB: I'll take a math question please.

CG: Awesome! The question is: What is 10 times 10?

(*Whitney rings in first*)

CJ: Whitney Whiney

Whitney: That's so easy! It's 20 of course!

CJ: I'm sorry but that's the incorrect answer.

Whitney: What?!

(CCC rings in)

CJ: Cocoa Chocolate Charlie

CCC: It's 100!!

CJ: That is 100 percent CORRECT! AWESOME!!

CCC: AWESOME!!!
CJ: AWESOME!

CCC: AWESOME!!!

CJ: Alright! Cocoa Chocolate Charlie, please select another category.

CCC: I'll take math again, please.

CJ: Awesome! The question is: If you buy lip-gloss for 75 cents, not saying you buy lip gloss Cocoa Chocolate Charlie, and pay the cashier with a one dollar bill, how much---

Whitney: One dollar and seventy five cents! YESS!!! YESS!!! YESSS!!!

CJ: That's some AWESOME adding Whitney, however, the last part of the question is, "how much change will you receive back?"

(Beautiful Bailey rings in)
BB: 25 cents!!

CJ: Well isn't that just awesome Beautiful Bailey! You are CORRECT!

Whitney: I don't understand why I can't answer any questions right...I mean, I thought I knew all this...

Boogie: Oh isn't it strange what you can learn, pay attention, maybe you'll get another turn!

Whitney: But Boogie, I don't understand! I know both of the other contestants! I got to school with them! Brittney Bonnet sits next to me in class and all she does is doodle hearts all the time. And Charlie over there, Charlie Checkers...all he cares about is hacky sac! He never studies!

Boogie: Never judge a book by it's cover, get to know people and see what you will uncover!

Whitney: But...

CJ: Ms. Bubblegum, please select a category.

BB: I'll take Language please.

CJ: Well that's just so awesome! The question is: How would you ask a teacher to use the restroom?

Whitney: EASY!! EASY EASY EASY!! "Excuse me, but can I please go to the bathroom?"

CCC: (*Laughing HYSTERICALLY*) OF COURSE YOU CAN GO TO THE BATHROOM!!!!! EVERYONE CAN GO TO THE BATHROOM!!!! THE CORRECT ANSWER IS MAY I PLEASE GO TO THE BATHROOM!

Whitney: Why is everyone laughing at me??? Stop it! Stop laughing! I just want my chocolate and then I want to go!

BBB: Maybe if you take more time with the questions you will answer them correctly.

Whitney: But Brittney...
BBB: Bailey

Whitney: Whatever. You don't even pay attention in class! All I ever see you doing is drawing hearts. How are you so smart when you don't study?

BBB: Whitney...I study all the time. Are you crazy? My mother would never let me watch T.V and play games if I didn't study

Whitney: Are you serious? I just thought you didn't care about school.

BBB: Of course I care about school. School is the most valuable tool we have. I love school!

Whitney: You LOVE school??

BBB: You bet chya! Or, I mean, I *did* love school, a long long time ago before I was princess (*cough*)

Here I'll help you with the next one. I think we have it. Cocoa Chocolate Charlie won't be answering the next one. He's too busy rolling around and laughing on the floor!

Whitney: Thanks..that's really nice of you!

CJ: Cocoa Chocolate Charlie you're pick.

CCC: (*laughing too hard to answer)*

CJ: Well then, it looks like Ms. Bubblegum, it's your pick.

BBB: (*consults with Whitney*) We'll take...I mean, I'll take, measurement.

CJ: Awesome! The question is: How many cups are in a pint?

Whitney: Oh no! I have no idea!

BBB: Haven't you ever helped your mom in the kitchen before??

Whitney: *(silent)* ...No I guess I haven't. Every time she asks I always say that I'm too busy making Valentines or doing something for my friends.

BBB: Oh Whitney. Cocoa Chocolate Charlie...we need to help our friend out.

(*The three contestants huddle. After a little discussion, Whitney buzzes in*)

Whitney: 2 cups!!! There are 2 cups in a pint!

CJ: Awesome!! You are correct Whitney! Your pick.

Whitney: I'll take math please

CJ: Ok Whitney, here's your question. If you have 12 candy hearts and your friend asks for 3 of them, how many candy hearts will you have left?

Whitney: Oh no, that's a hard one.

CCC: YOU CAN DO IT WHITNEY!

Whitney: I'm not so sure I can...

BBB: Sure you can, Whitney. Just use the hearts in my kingdom to help you. Look over there at that wall. There are 12 hearts on that wall. Hey C-Sauce! Go eat three!

CCC: OK!!!!!!

BBB: Now Whitney, how many are left?

Whitney: (Whitney counts) 9!!! There are NINE hearts left!

CJ: Correct! 100 percent correct!
Awesome Whitney! 11 percent awesome!

Whitney: Thanks, Brittney, I mean Bailey..you're a true friend.

Whitney: Wow, I never realized how important education was before. I guess I always took what I was learning in school for granted! Ha-ha but as it turns out, learning can be fun! As long as you work hard and support your friends!

CJ: The next question goes to Whitney.

Whitney: Why don't you pick BBB.

BBB: Ok, I'll take the wild card

CCC: WILDCARD WILDCARD!!! HAHAHA!

CJ: Beautiful Bailey, your question is: What is the color of the character Shrek?
BBB: Oh no! I have no idea! I have never seen that movie! I'm always reading!

Whitney: Don't worry, Bailey. I'll help you. I've seen Shrek tons of times!

Think of grass, think of broccoli, think of spinach think of...

BBB: Green!

CJ: Correct! Awesome!

(The three contestants exchange high fives!) (A bell is heard)

CJ: That sound means the game is up....and we have some GREAT news!

Due to the AWESOME team work we saw today, everyone is a winner! United Unicorn, bring them their prize!

(*United Unicorn brings out the box of chocolate. The three contestants start eating)*

Boogie: *(Dancing*) Oh what excitement oh what pizzazz, this just makes me what to sing some jazz. Look how friendship really begins, and look over there, nothing but grins. This game show sure taught Whitney the importance of education, and look, no more frustration!

(The lights come down on the three sharing the box of chocolates and Boogie dancing around onstage.)

SCENE 3:

Lights up on Whitney sleeping in her bed. We see her tossing and turning. All of a sudden Whitney starts laughing and wakes herself up. Her mom comes in to see what all the commotion is.

Mom: Whitney! What on earth is the matter!?

Whitney: Oh mom! (*runs and gives her mom a great big hug!)* I'm so sorry for not studying! From now on, I will respect my teachers and the assignments they give me! I now know how lucky I am to be getting such a great education! From now on, all I 'm going to do is study study study!!

Mom: Ha-ha oh Whitney! What has come over you? I mean, this is really very wonderful, but, what brought on such a change?

Whitney: Let's just say: A little friend came my way, and showed me truly the right game to play. While I learned that I didn't answer any questions right, some friends came along but not to fight. They helped me understand the true meaning of education, and now I know, it is the only salvation!

Mom: Oh Whitney! You always surprise me!

Whitney: AWESOME! Isn't it just AWESOME, mom??!

Mom: Ha-ha Oh yes, Whitney, this is very awesome!

Whitney: I'm going to do my homework right now!

Mom: Ok honey, then I'll say goodnight. Don't stay up to late. (*gives Whitney a hug and kiss then exits)*

Whitney goes to her backpack to take out her books and finds a Heart filled with chocolate!

Whitney: Awesome!

The lights go down on Whitney eating chocolate and studying.

The Secret Cave
By Anna Isaacson

Anna is the daughter of Title 1 teacher Kari Isaacson

This story has been passed down on my mom's side of the family for 4 generations.

My great-great-great-grandparents, Edwin and Bertha Tollefson, moved to the United States in the mid-1800s from Norway. According to Norwegian tradition, only the first-born son inherited the family land, and since Edwin was the second or third son in his family, he and his new wife, Bertha, decided to immigrate to the United States. They settled in a tiny Minnesota town called Belfast in the center of the state, where the land was both fertile and expensive: perfect for an immigrating family with not a penny to their name.

Edwin and Bertha had many children to help with the farming, and their youngest was Dora, who would later become my great-great-grandmother. When Dora was 3 years old, the year was 1862, and the Sioux Indians, led by Chief Little Crow and aided by the M'dekakanton Indians, went on a massacring spree through Minnesota. They would burn the fields and homes of innocent villagers, and kill everybody in their path. Entire towns were burned to the ground, with no survivors.

When Chief Little Crow had destroyed a neighboring town, the people of Belfast knew they had to act quickly, or else their town, too, would be demolished. Some of the men went in search of a hideout where they could flee to in case the Indians came. They searched and searched, when finally one of the men's son told him about a secret cave where he and his friends would often play. It was only accessible by swimming into it from under the nearby lake, and it was nearly impossible to know it wasn't just an ordinary rock formation. This cave was sure to save the people in the town.

Sure enough, the screams of the Indians were heard approaching Belfast late one night, so the people of the town alerted one another and they silently fled to the lake and swam to their secret hiding place. They stayed in the cave all night and when morning came, they cautiously emerged to see what was left of their homes. Belfast's fate was the same as that of the other towns Chief Little Crow had attacked. Not one building was left un-charred, and all of the crops were destroyed. Everything the people of Belfast had worked so hard for was gone, but not one person was killed, thanks to the secret cave. The other victims of the massacres were not so lucky: altogether, nearly 650 villagers were killed.

El Nacimiento de Mi Herman

Por Saúl Cuautle y Georgina Cielo

Cuando yo tenía 5 años, deseaba tener un hermanito porque mis primos que viven en México tenían sus hermanitos y yo no. Por eso quiera a alguien con quien jugar y no estar solo. Entonces le pedí a mama y a papa un hermanito y a si fue. Después de mucho tiempo supe que en lo pansita de mama había un bebe y me puse muy contento. Entonces, empecé a pensar come se iba a llamar y todo los nombres que yo oía en cualquier parte se asian bonitos para mi hermanito o hermanita que venia en camino.

The Birth of My Brother

When I was 5 years old, I wanted to have a brother because my cousins who live in Mexico had their brothers and not me. That's why I wanted someone to play with and not be alone.

So, I asked my mama and papa for a brother and it happened. After a long time I learned that there was a baby in my mother's stomach and I was very happy. Then I started thinking what we would call him. All the names I heard everywhere sounded pretty for my brother or sister who would come soon.

Mi Cumpleanos

Por Saul Cuautle y Georgina Cielo

En el mes de febrero es mi cumpleaños y estaba muy emocionado porque mi mama me dijo que me lo iba a festejar. Semanas antes fuimos a comprar todo para mi fiesta, como juegos, piñata, las invitaciones, globos, platos, vasos, antifaces. Toda la casa se decoro de la película los Increíbles. Invite a todos mis amigos y amigas. Llego el día y estaba muy contento. Me prepare muy temprano y estaba listo para recibir mi fiesta con todos. Después mi tía Jessica, me preparo un pastel muy bonito que también fue de los Increíbles. Me gusto mucho.

My Birthday

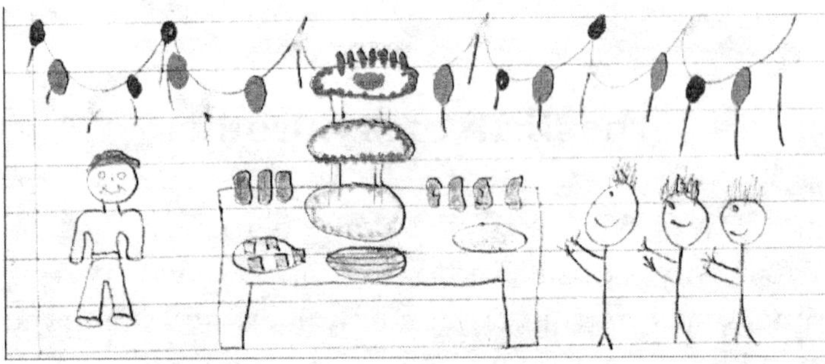

The month of February is my birthday and I was very excited because my mother told me that she would have a party for me. Weeks before we went to buy all the things for my party like, games, a piñata, invitations, balloons, plates, cups and masks. The whole house was decorated like the movie "The Incredibles". I invited all my friends. The day came and I was very happy. I got ready early and was ready to receive my party with all my friends. My Aunt Jessica made me a very pretty cake that was also decorated like "The Incredibles". I liked it very much.

PATH TO HOPE

by Karin and Erin Brown

Hope Elementary school was a wonderful school, with caring teaches and terrific kids. The school was in a nice community in a very big city. Behind the school was a nursing home, some people call them old age homes, it was a place where old people went to live that needed tobe taken care of.

Before and after school many children would take a short cut to main street. They would climb through a large hole in the fence behind the school playground and walk through the nursing home grounds to the main street. It was a much quicker way home for most of the school kids.

Shannon took the shortcut home every day with two of her brothers, James and

Carson, her older brother Dan was in high school. All through the school year children walked through the nursing home grounds. Every day the old people would look forward to seeing them. In the morning they waved through the window while they were having their breakfast. When the weather was warm they often sat outside waiting for the children toget out of school, the kids would share pictures they had drawn, and stories of their day, the old people would often share stories of their past when they were young. Even when the weather was cold they would wave at each other, the children enjoyed the old people and they enjoyed the children.

Even though the ursing home was not school or city property, nobody seemed to mind the kids walking through every day. The school principle Mrs. Cline had always overlooked the fact that the kids walked through the nursing home grounds, after all the hole in the fence had been there as long as anyone could remember. Mrs. Cline's own father had stayed in that very nursing home before he passed away and she remembered how he had enjoyed the children.

One summer a new head nurse Victoria came to run the nursing home, she did not like the hole in the fence or the dirt path that had been worn in the grass over the years, she thought it looked muddy and messy. The other staff members at the nursing home explained to her how the children from Hoe Elementary walked to and from school through the nursing home property. She did not like that one bit, "The last thing we need at this nursing home is a bunch of bratty kids bothering the poor old people who live here." That summer she had a new fence put up and a large sign that said NO TRESSPASSING! Net she wrote a letter to the principal Mrs. Cline making it very clear that she did not want children walking through the nursing home grounds anymore.

Shannon and her brothers were very sad when they returned to school in the fall to find the new fence and the large NO TRESSPASSING SIGN. She had really been looking forward to seeing Beatrice, her good friend who lived in the nursing home, she had pictures of her summer vacation to show her and a necklace she had made at camp.

Shannon, James and Carson walked home the long way after school that day. When they arrived home they told their older brother Dan about the shortcut being gone. Dan was very sad for them, he had fond memories of all the old people he had come to know during his years at Hope elementary. Sometimes on Saturday he would go visit his friend Otto, an old man who lived at the nursing home. He always brought Otto cookies and Otto would tell him stories about growing up on a farm in the olden days. Dan had always lived in the city and really enjoyed Otto's farm stories. Dan told Shannon he would take her to the nursing home this Saturday so she could visit Beatrice.

Saturday finally arrived and Dan and Shannon walked down Maine Street to the nursing home. They stopped at the bakery to get Otto's favorite cookies. When they arrived at the nursing home they found their friends Otto and Beatrice sitting outside as it was a beautiful September day. They wee excited to see Shannon and Dan and told them how much everybody missed seeing the children. Beatrice told Shannon that all of the people in the nursing home had been sad to find out about the fence and the NO TRESPASSING sign. Beatrice said they had nothing to look forward to in their day now that the fence was up and the path was closed. When it was time to say goodbye to their friends they promised to come back the next week.

The very next Saturday while Shannon and Dan walked to the nursing home down Main Street they saw a big sign posted in the bakery window it said SAVE OUR SKATEBOARD PARK. When they walked into the bakery to buy Otto's cookies Mr. Ballard the baker asked them if they would sign his daughter's petition. "What's a petition? asked Shannon. Mr. Ballard explained to them that a petition was a collection of signatures to prove that the majority of people in the town felt strongly about something. He told them that his daughter Brooke and her friends had been collecting signatures so that the skateboard park where they skated would not be torn down by the city. Dan and Shannon agreed to sign the petition and as they were signing they both had the same wonderful idea.

Over the next week Shannon, Dan, James and Carson gathered together with many of their friends. They started a SAVE THE NURSING HOME PATH petition. Every person old and young in the community was signing like crazy, they all knew how the shortcut had been there for as long as anyone could remember and it was more than just a quick way to and from school, it brought friendship between young and old people.

The following Saturday they presented the petition to the head nurse Victoria. She admitted that since she had closed the path by having a new fence put up, everybody had been angry with her. Her neighbors wouldn't talk to her and her good friend had thrown a garden party and didn't even invite her. Victoria agreed to reopen the fence but only if the community could raise enough money to have it paved properly, and have a gate instead of a hole in the fence.

The whole community got to work right away. They had a carnival at the school to raise money, with games, crafts and a bake sale. Many local businesses donated money and equipment including benches, gardening equipment, plants and flowers. When the project was complete they had a ceremony at the entrance to path the path on Main Street. Shannon and Beatrice held hands and cut the ribbon at the paths entrance.

The path has been completed now for many years, and is enjoyed all year long by young and old. Even in the summer when the kids are out of school they ride bikes, roller skate and walk along the path that runs through the nursing home grounds. The old people share stories about the past and in their friendship with the children they hold hope for the future. At the entrance to the path of Main Street is a small garden with a sign that reads

THE PATH TO HOPE PLEASE TRESPASS.

THE PERFECT DAY

by Teresa Lone

dedicated to my family

My family is so busy sometimes we need a day to reconnect as a family. I want to tell you about my perfect day, it begins with me waking up to my 3 year old Matthew, my 11 year old Jamie and my husband Jim having a deep discussion on how to make pancakes quietly so they don't wake me up. I get up we all make Mickey Mouse pancakes. We eat pancakes and talk about what we are going to do together, we end up back in my bed reading our favorite books to each other. After a couple hours of that we get dressed and go outside and play in the sand box and the trampoline. Then we lay on a blanket and look up at the clouds and discover a whole new world of Bunny Robbit, Dinosaur and castles in the clouds. Then we have a teddy be a picnic in the front yard with all the Peanut Butter Sandwiches you can eat.

Then we go for a hike in the woods. We watch the squirrels play in the trees above us and listen to the birds sing. Matthew discovers a new green but to scare his sister with. Jamie found a new rock for her collection. Jim discovered he is still young enough to climb a tree and act like a monkey. I enjoyed taking my shoes off and wading in the creek with my children, like I did when I was a little girl. Then we go back to our house and we all get comfortable on the couch and watch Finding Nemo. We have these perfect days at least twice a month. The story may vary but the results are the same. We connect as a family and when my days get hectic and stressed I remember one of those perfect days.

Sharks

By Mahmood Mahmoodi

Most people think that sharks eat humans but they are wrong. The only reason why people think that sharks eat humans is because they see it in movies. Sharks eat humans sometimes, in accident because they think that when surfers are on their surf boards they look like seals. Seals are one of the sharks favorite foods.

When sharks hunt their prey they have something in their eyes that protects them from getting hurt. There are over 90 different kids of sharks in the world. The most dangerous of them all is the Great White Shark. Sharks are really fast, they can go over 30 MPH.
The biggest shark is the whale shark. It has blue skin and white dots all over it. It does not attack humans at all.

You may be wondering why do all sharks have scars all over them. It is because when sharks are young they get beat up by some of the mad sharks. Sharks can smell a tiny drop of blood from over one mile away because of their strong sense of smell. If you get close to a shark or touch the top of their skin you will bleed because on top of their skin it is rough but at the bottom of their skin it is really soft. Sharks can go without food for a long time. They are very strong. Shark food is really famous in some countries.

A long time ago people got some kind of medicine from sharks. People in other countries kill sharks for their skins. People can make lots of stuff from sharks that are expensive. Scientists once found nails, jewelry, needles, boxes, cans and spears. Sharks are one of the strongest predators under the water. Sharks are found to be a threat to other animals under the water.

In Our Family We Have Five Pets

By Emma, Hillary, Allison, and Tom Walsh

In our family we have five pets: three cats and two rabbits. We used to have two hamsters and before that we had fish. Our cats are Dexter, Ivy, and Ella. Our rabbits are Butterscotch and Daisy.

Dexter is a gray cat and she is 17 years old. Ivy is a yellow cat and she is 15 years old. Ella is a calico cat and she is 3 years old. Butterscotch is butterscotch and white. He is 2 years old. When you look at Daisy, she looks brown, but when you run your fingers through her fur you can see dark brown, light brown, black, white, and gray. She is also 2 years old.

We found Dexter through a classified ad in Nashville, Tennessee. Ivy was found by our neighbor in the middle of Fifth Street here in Bloomington. We didn't think we needed a second cat, but we thought Dexter might want a friend. Ella's mama, Belle, showed up at Grandmey and Grandad's house in the woods and decided that was a good place to have her babies—five of them. We didn't think we needed a third cat, but Grandmey picked out Ella just for us and we couldn't resist.

We got Butterscotch from a rabbit breeder in New Albany, Indiana. He is a cross between two breeds of rabbit—lionhead and Netherland dwarf. Lionheads have long hair around their heads, like a lion's mane, but Butterscotch doesn't have a mane.

Daisy came from a young girl who was just getting started as a breeder. She's a Mini Rex and she's as soft as a cloud.

Dexter is named after jazz saxophonist Dexter Gordon. He was a man and everyone thinks our Dexter is a boy, but she's not. Ivy is named after jazz singer Ivie Anderson.

Ella was named by Grandmey, and Ella is also the name of a great jazz singer—Ella Fitzgerald. Hillary and Emma chose the names for their rabbits, Butterscotch and Daisy, because those were the names they liked best.

Our cats are indoor cats. They never go outside. The rabbits don't go outside either. They have large cages in the family room. Each cage has a hutch, a litter box, a food bowl, a water bottle, and toys hanging from the top bars.

Dexter, Ivy, and Ella like cat treats. The treats smell bad! But they mostly eat cat food.
Butterscotch and Daisy love to eat raisins, and sometimes vegetable treats. But they mostly eat green leaf lettuce, parsley, carrots, and hay.

Dexter likes to chase paper wads and take naps on Mommy. Ivy likes to spill her water and drink it off the floor. Ella likes to chase string and lie in the sun.

Butterscotch likes to sit on top of his hutch. Daisy likes to eat.

Dexter gets mad when you talk about her. She puts her ears sideways and frowns. Ivy gets mad when Ella attacks her. She swats at her with her front paws. Ella gets mad if you bother her when she wants to be left alone. She yowls like someone is pulling her tail. When Butterscotch gets mad, he thumps his back feet, and sometimes he grunts. Daisy gets mad if you put your hand in her cage while she's eating. She grunts and charges, but she doesn't bite.

When Dexter is happy, she purrs and purrs. When Ivy is happy, she nudges your hand to make you pet her. When Ella is happy, she winds around your legs and tries to get your attention. When Butterscotch and Daisy are happy, they do big, happy hops in the air.

When Dexter feels funny, she chases her tail. When Ivy feels funny, she rolls on her back on the floor. When Ella feels funny, she runs across the room fast and leaps into the air. And then she does it again. When Butterscotch feels funny, he lets us play hide and seek with him. When Daisy feels funny, she runs fast around the couch and two chairs, over and over again.

Sometimes three cats feel like a lot of cats, but we still wish we had more. Sometimes two rabbits feel like a lot of rabbits, but we still wish we had more. But five pets make a lot of laughter and love.

Moving through Time

By Forrest DeFelice and Anne Gardner

A baby
A year old
Mom and Dad live separately
Meeting Anne for the first time
I don't remember before I knew her

A toddler
Running through the park
Visiting Anne and Dad in the evenings
Living with Mom
My sister
My Brother

A preschooler
Cutting my curly locks
At the play dough table
Becoming a big brother
River

A kindergartner
Making friends
Cutting out pictures of classmates
Glued onto a piece of paper

On the eve of first grade
Just seven years old,
Starting a new life
New home
New family
Living with Anne and Dad

Second grade
Gallagher's guitar
Kids singing
Making my way
Anne teaches at my school

Third grade
Nine years old
Thinking I was going to get a sister
And losing an old stepfather

Fourth grade
Divorced again
Anne and Dad
Anne became my custodial parent
Talking to think and feel
Working late at school

Fifth grade
Starts with Anne
And then my dad
His home
Two bachelors
Drinking milk out of the carton

The future,
Sixth grade and beyond
Middle school
High school
College
Whatever is in store for me
I'll meet it soon
Arms open